First Guide to Government

What Are the Amendments?

Nancy Harris

Heinemann Library
Chicago, IL

HEINEMANN-RAINTREE

TO ORDER:
☎ Phone Customer Service **888-454-2279**
💻 Visit **www.heinemannraintree.com** to browse our catalog and order online.

©2008 Heinemann-Raintree
a division of Capstone Global Library, LLC
Chicago, Illinois

Editorial: Rebecca Rissman
Design: Kimberly R. Miracle and Betsy Wernert
Illustrations: Mapping Specialists
Photo Research: Tracy Cummins and Heather Mauldin
Production: Duncan Gilbert

Originated by Modern Age
Printed and bound in Stevens Point, Wisconsin.
The paper used to print this book comes from sustainable resources.

ISBN-13: 978-1-4329-0986-4 (hc)
ISBN-10: 1-4329-0986-X (hc)
ISBN-13: 978-1-4329-0992-5 (pb)
ISBN-10: 1-4329-0992-4 (pb)

052012
006738

Library of Congress
Cataloging-in-Publication Data
Harris, Nancy.
  What are the amendments? / Nancy Harris. -- 1st ed.
    p. cm. -- (First guide to government)
  Includes bibliographical references and index.
  ISBN 978-1-4329-0986-4 (hc) -- ISBN 978-1-4329-0992-5 (pb) 1. Constitutional amendments--United States--Juvenile literature. 2. Constitutional history--United States--Juvenile literature. 3. Civil rights--United States--Juvenile literature. I. Title.
  KF4555.H37 2008
  342.7303--dc22
                    2008001152

Acknowledgments
The author and publisher are grateful to the following for permission to reproduce copyright material: ©AP Photo **pp. 23** (The Morning Sun/Andrew D. Brosig), **28** (Charles Dharapak); ©ASSOCIATED PRESS **p. 15**; ©Corbis **pp. 4** (Tetra Images), **13** (Matthew Cavanaugh), **22** (Brettmann), **29** (Gregg Newton); ©Getty Images **pp. 6** (Congressional Quarterly), **10** (Alex Wong), **24** (AFP/MANDL NGAN), **27**; ©Library of Congress Prints and Photographs Division **p. 26**; ©The National Archives and Records Administration **pp. 5, 9, 18**; ©North Wind Picture Archives **p. 20** (North Wind); ©Redux **p. 17** (The New York Times/Brendan Smialowski); ©REUTERS **p. 14** (Mike Theiler); ©Shutterstock **p. 12** (Arvind Balaraman); ©The Granger Collection, New York **pp. 8, 16, 19, 21**.

Cover images used with permission of ©Library of Congress Prints and Photographs Division and ©The National Archives and Records Administration.

The publishers would like to thank Nancy Harris for her assistance in the preparation of this book.

Every effort has been made to contact copyright holders of any material reproduced in this book. Any omissions will be rectified in subsequent printings if notice is given to the publisher.

Disclaimer
All the Internet addresses (URLs) given in this book were valid at the time of going to press. However, due to the dynamic nature of the Internet, some addresses may have changed, or sites may have changed or ceased to exist since publication. While the author and publisher regret any inconvenience this may cause readers, no responsibility for any such changes can be accepted by either the author or the publisher.

Contents

Some words are shown in bold, **like this**. You can find out what they mean by looking in the glossary.

What Is the United States Constitution?

The United States Constitution is a very important **document** (paper). It is a written **law** (rule) that must be followed by everyone in the United States. The Constitution explains how the **federal government** works. The United States federal government leads the whole country.

The Constitution created the United States government.

The United States Constitution has three parts. The first part is the **preamble**. This section tells why the Constitution was written. The second part is the **articles**. The articles describe how the United States federal government must work. The third part is the amendments. These are changes that have been made to the Constitution.

5

Why Do We Have the Amendments?

★★★ The Constitution allows congresspeople to make or change laws.

The amendments make the United States Constitution a special document. They mean that the Constitution can be changed to meet the needs of people in the United States. The Constitution can be changed at any time.

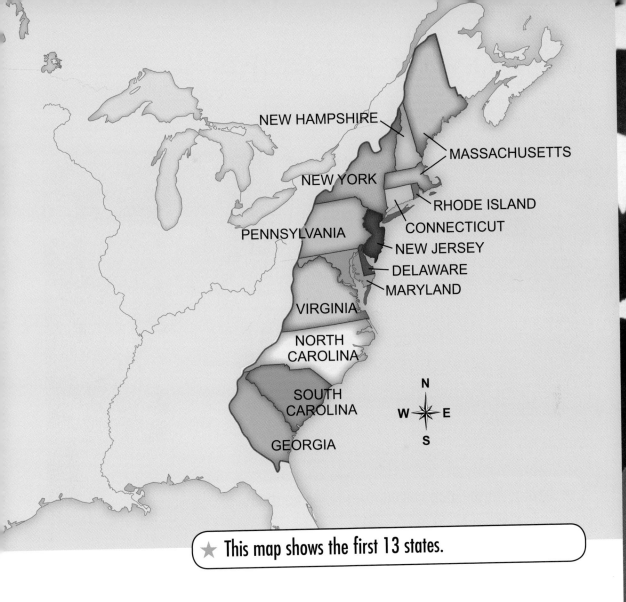

NEW HAMPSHIRE

MASSACHUSETTS

NEW YORK

RHODE ISLAND

CONNECTICUT

PENNSYLVANIA

NEW JERSEY

DELAWARE

MARYLAND

VIRGINIA

NORTH CAROLINA

SOUTH CAROLINA

GEORGIA

N
W E
S

★ This map shows the first 13 states.

The United States Constitution was written in 1787. At that time, the United States was a new country. There were only 13 states. Today there are 50 states.

★ George Washington helped to write the Constitution.

The men who wrote the Constitution knew the country would become larger. They knew the needs of the country would change as the country grew. They wanted the Constitution to meet the needs of the country as it changed.

When these men wrote the Constitution, they included an **article** to address this need. Article Five explains how changes can be made to the Constitution.

★ There are seven original articles in the Constitution.

How to Amend the Constitution

The authors of the Constitution did not want it to be easy to change. They wanted people to think hard before changing the **law** of the Constitution. A lot of people have to agree to any amendment to the Constitution.

Extend the Deadline
End the Penalty
Fix Part D

Extend the Deadline

Fix Part D

★★★ New York Representative Charles Rangel holds a rally to tell people about a new law.

One way to add an amendment to the Constitution is through the United States **federal government**. The federal government has three branches (parts). Each branch of the federal government has a certain job.

★ Congress meets in the Capitol Building in Washington, D.C.

The **legislative branch** makes **laws** for the entire country. People who work in the legislative branch work in **Congress**. The people who work in Congress can **amend** (change) the Constitution.

★ Senator Hillary Clinton works in Congress.

First the people in Congress come up with an idea for a new law to be added to the Constitution. This idea is called a **bill**. The bill is then shown to everyone in Congress.

★ There are 535 people in the United States Congress.

For a **bill** to be approved, two-thirds of the people in **Congress** must vote in favor of the bill. If this happens, the bill is sent to each state's government.

Leaders in each state's government then vote on the bill. If three-fourths of the states vote in favor of the bill, it is approved. The new **law** is added as an **amendment** to the Constitution.

★ This is a state government meeting.

The First Ten Amendments

The first ten amendments are called the **Bill of Rights**. They were added only four years after the Constitution had been written. The Bill of Rights was added to protect the rights of people living in the United States. Rights are freedoms that people have.

★★★ The Bill of Rights was ratified (approved) in 1791.

Some of these rights include the right to speak or write what you believe. They include the right to be treated fairly if you are accused of breaking a law. Many of the authors of the Constitution felt it was important to add these amendments.

★★★ The freedom of speech allows Americans to rally or protest for what they believe.

Other Amendments

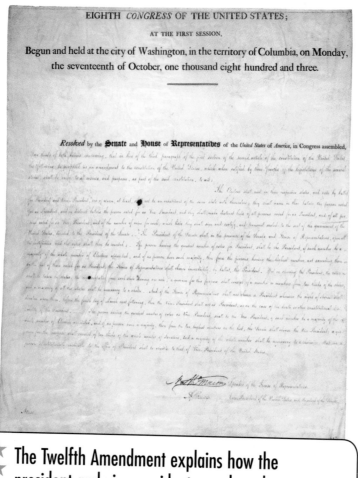

EIGHTH *CONGRESS* OF THE UNITED STATES;

AT THE FIRST SESSION,

Begun and held at the city of Washington, in the territory of Columbia, on Monday, the seventeenth of October, one thousand eight hundred and three.

★ ★ ★ The Twelfth Amendment explains how the president and vice president are elected.

As the country grew, more amendments were added. The amendments show what important things were happening in the country at that time. They show how people's ideas and beliefs were changing.

The Thirteenth Amendment

The Thirteenth Amendment was added in 1865. This amendment said you could not own slaves. Up until then, it was not against the law to own slaves. Slaves were not paid and were told what to do by their owners. The Thirteenth Amendment freed people who had been slaves.

★ This is a group of freed slaves in Virginia.

There were people who did not agree with the Thirteenth Amendment. They did not like that slaves were now free. They did not want to treat the freed slaves as **citizens**.

★★★ People in Tennessee burned a school to show that they were angry slaves were becoming citizens.

⭐⭐⭐ In 1870 the Fifteenth Amendment granted freed slaves the right to vote.

The Fourteenth and Fifteenth Amendments

The Fourteenth and Fifteenth Amendments were added to protect the newly freed slaves. The Fourteenth Amendment made the freed slaves citizens. The Fifteenth Amendment gave them the right to vote for leaders.

★ These women are voting for the first time.

The Nineteenth Amendment

The Nineteenth Amendment was added to give all **citizens** the right to vote. It was added in 1920. Before that time women were not allowed to vote. This amendment is famous for giving women the right to vote.

Women had been trying to get the right to vote for years. Some states let women vote before 1920. After the Nineteenth Amendment was added, all women finally had the right to vote in the United States.

★ All American citizens can vote after the age of 18.

The Twenty-Third Amendment

The Twenty-Third Amendment gave **citizens** who lived in the District of Columbia the right to vote for federal leaders. Before this amendment was added, they could not vote for president and vice president of the United States. The Twenty-Third Amendment was added in 1961.

> ★★★ The District of Columbia can vote for federal leaders. But, it is not represented in Congress.

24

The District of Columbia is not a state. It is the capital of the United States and is where federal leaders work.

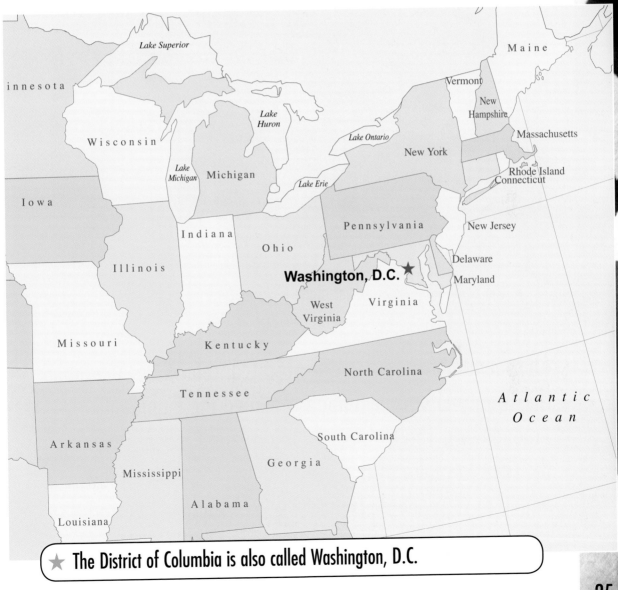

★ The District of Columbia is also called Washington, D.C.

Repealing Amendments

★ The Eighteenth Amendment made it illegal to drink alcohol.

An amendment can be **repealed** (canceled). For example, the Twenty-First Amendment repealed the Eighteenth Amendment. The Eighteenth Amendment made it against the **law** to make or buy alcoholic beverages. This law was added to stop people from drinking alcoholic beverages such as beer, liquor, or wine. It was added in 1919.

★ The Twenty-First Amendment made alcohol legal again.

The Twenty-First Amendment gave back the rights people had lost with the Eighteenth Amendment. They could now make or purchase alcoholic beverages if they were of legal age. The Twenty-First Amendment was added in 1933.

Why Are the Amendments Important?

Many ideas for new amendments are talked about each year in **Congress**. Very few are approved. Currently there are only 27 amendments to the Constitution.

★ This senator is explaining a bill to the Senate.

★ You can view the Constitution in Washington, D.C.

The United States Constitution is the highest law in the United States. The amendments are an important part of this **document**. They mean that the Constitution can be changed over time to meet the needs of United States **citizens**.

Glossary

amend change a piece of text. You can amend the constitution by adding a new law.

article part or piece of writing in a text. There are articles in the US Constitution.

bill written proposal or idea for a new law. A law is a rule people must obey in a state or in the country.

Bill of Rights first ten amendments. These changes were added to protect the rights (freedoms) of people who live in the United States.

citizen person who is born in the United States. People who have moved to the United States from another country can become citizens by taking a test.

Congress group of people who made the laws for the entire country. Two groups of people work in Congress. They are called the Senate and the House of Representatives. Congress is the legislative branch in the United States federal government.

document written text or paper. The United States Constitution is a document.

federal government group of leaders who run the entire country. In a federal government, the country is made up of many states.

law rule people must obey in a state or country

legislative branch part of the United States federal government that makes laws. Congress is the legislative branch.

Preamble first part of a text. It is written to tell why the paper was written.

repeal get rid of, change, or cancel a law

state government group of leaders who run a particular state. Each state in the United States has a state government.

Find Out More

Books to Read

An older reader can help you with these books:

Crewe, Sabrina and Anderson, Dale. *The Seneca Falls Women's Rights Convention*. Milwaukee, WI: Gareth Stevens Publishing, 2005.

Pearl, Norman. *The Bill of Rights*. Mankato, MN: Picture Window Books, 2007.

Teitelbaum, Michael. *The U.S. Constitution*. Mankato, MN: Child's World, 2005.

Websites

Ben's Guide to U.S. Government
Visit **http://bensguide.gpo.gov/** to play games and learn the ABCs of the United States Government.

Viewing the US Constitution

The US Constitution is on display in the National Archives in the Rotunda. The Rotunda is open daily from 9 am to 5 pm.

The National Archives address is:
700 Pennsylvania Avenue, NW
Washington, DC 20408

Index